Dr. Chuck Tingle's
Adult Coloring And Activity Book
For True Buckaroos

ISBN: 1546649646
ISBN-13: 978-1546649649

DEDICATION

I dedicate this book to all of the buckaroos out there fighting to prove love is real every single day.

TRAIN YOUR BRAIN

We all know that an active mind keeps a buckaroo healthy and wise. In an effort to keep your butts and brains sharp, I have created this powerful coloring and activity book. Please enjoy these pages specifically designed to unlock your creative potential, and to put a hop in your trot as your navigate this timeline with real buckaroo love. Color this book in a way that is uniquely you, because your way is the most special and important way of all.

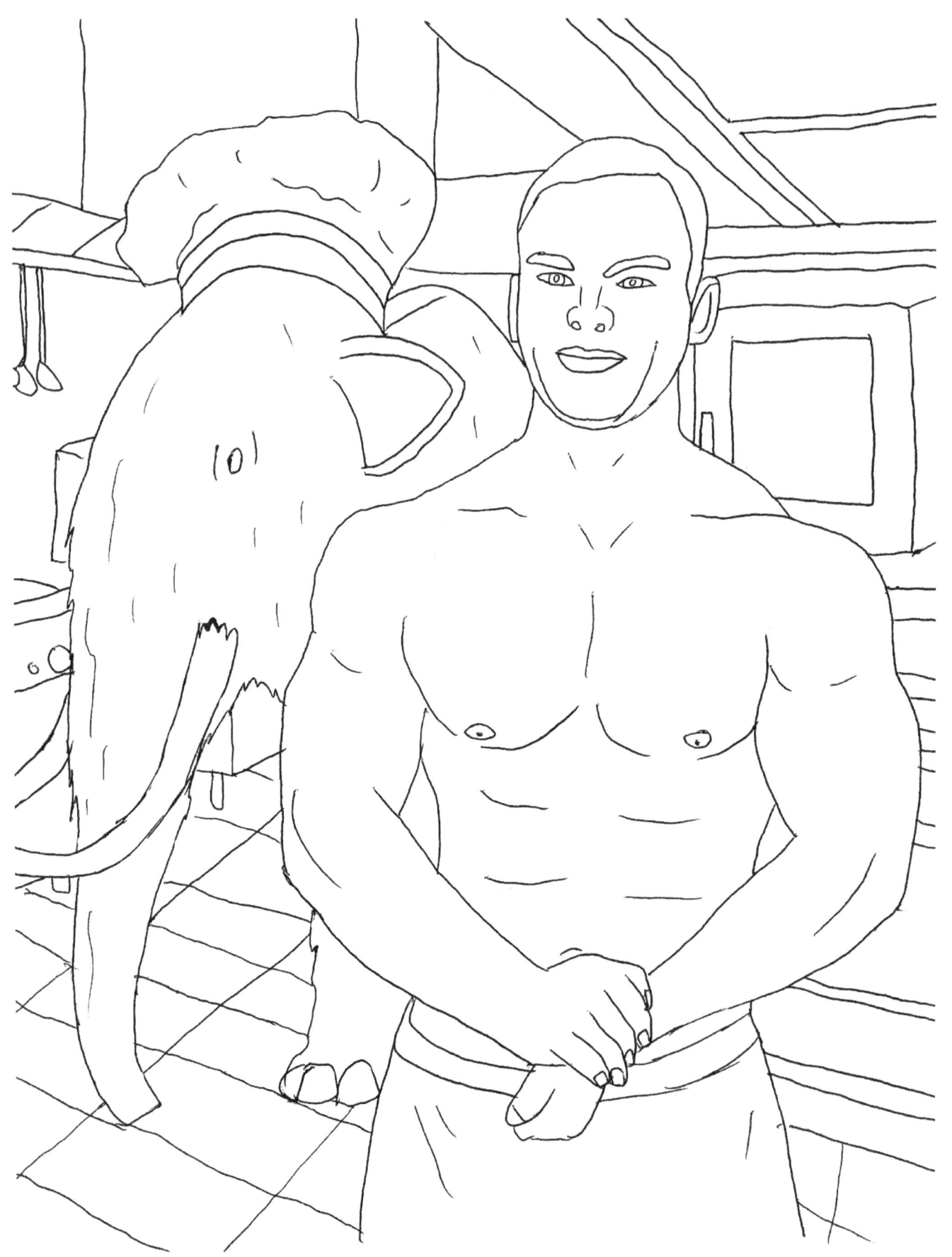

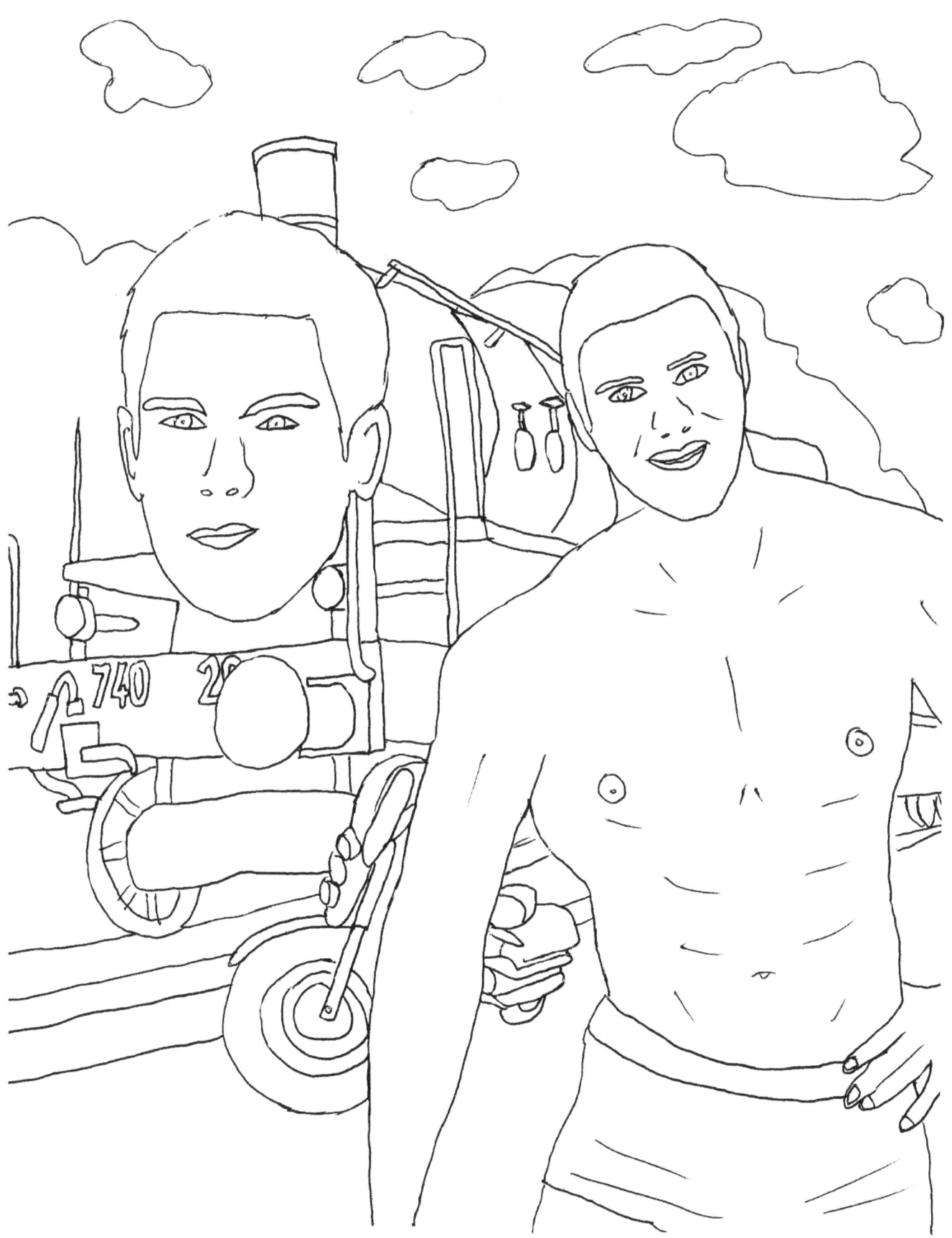

Please enjoy this important Tingleverse crossword puzzle.

DOWN:

1. Universally regarded as the world's greatest beverage.
2. Hit film starring Channing Tatum. Subtitle: A Dancer's Dream Story.
3. 2-ply is safety standard for these important suits.
4. Lorko does this to your balls in a classic tingler.
5. School of magic that puts a spring in your step and makes you feel good.
6. Truckman's favorite activity.
8. A vast, empty place located outside all layers of reality.
10. Contemporary alternative to traditional horseplay.
12. Best thing to do with your body in the dark.
13. _____ newspaper, The New York Times.
16. Gay T-Rex Law Firm: Executive _____.
18. In order to prove love, it is important to keep your eyes, heart, and butt in this way.
19. Dinosaur hero of the classic tingler, Space Raptor Butt Invasion.
22. This neighbor belongs in a snake pit.

ACROSS

7. Lonesome vehicle with a haunting way that often comes at night.
9. Hollywood's other name.
11. The one true rule across all timelines.
14. The four types of tinglers are: bigfoot, dinosaur, unicorn and _____.
15. Night bus number 13 is more than just a living vehicle, his is one of these.
17. Home of Sweet Barbara.
20. What Sweet Barbara sounds like when she stands at the foot of your bed.
21. Birthplace of Dr. Chuck Tingle.
24. Something that we all know.
26. Old time phrase: Hawks on a _____.
27. The world's most handsome son.

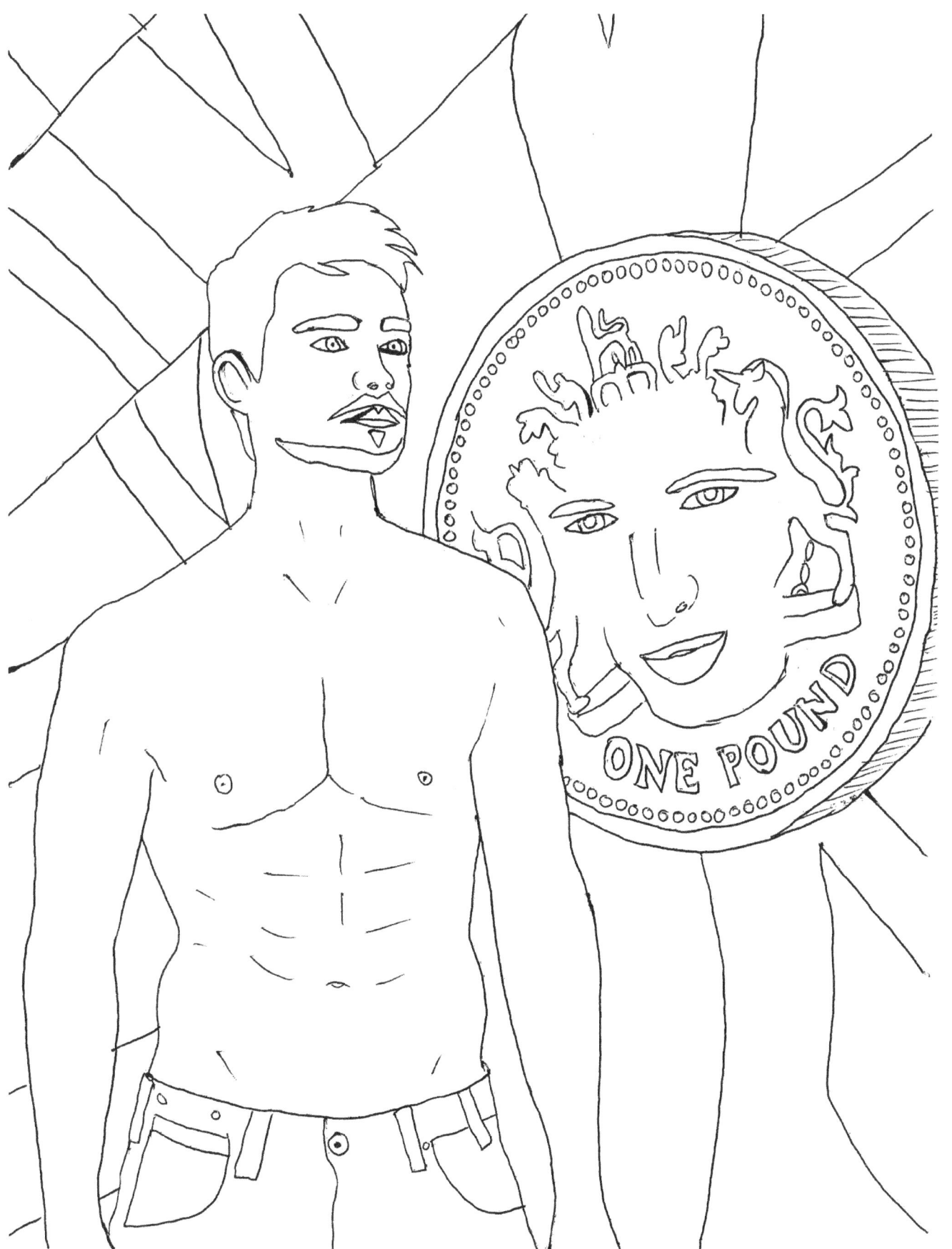

Help Sweet Barbara get home by taking the right path and avoiding the frozen lake!

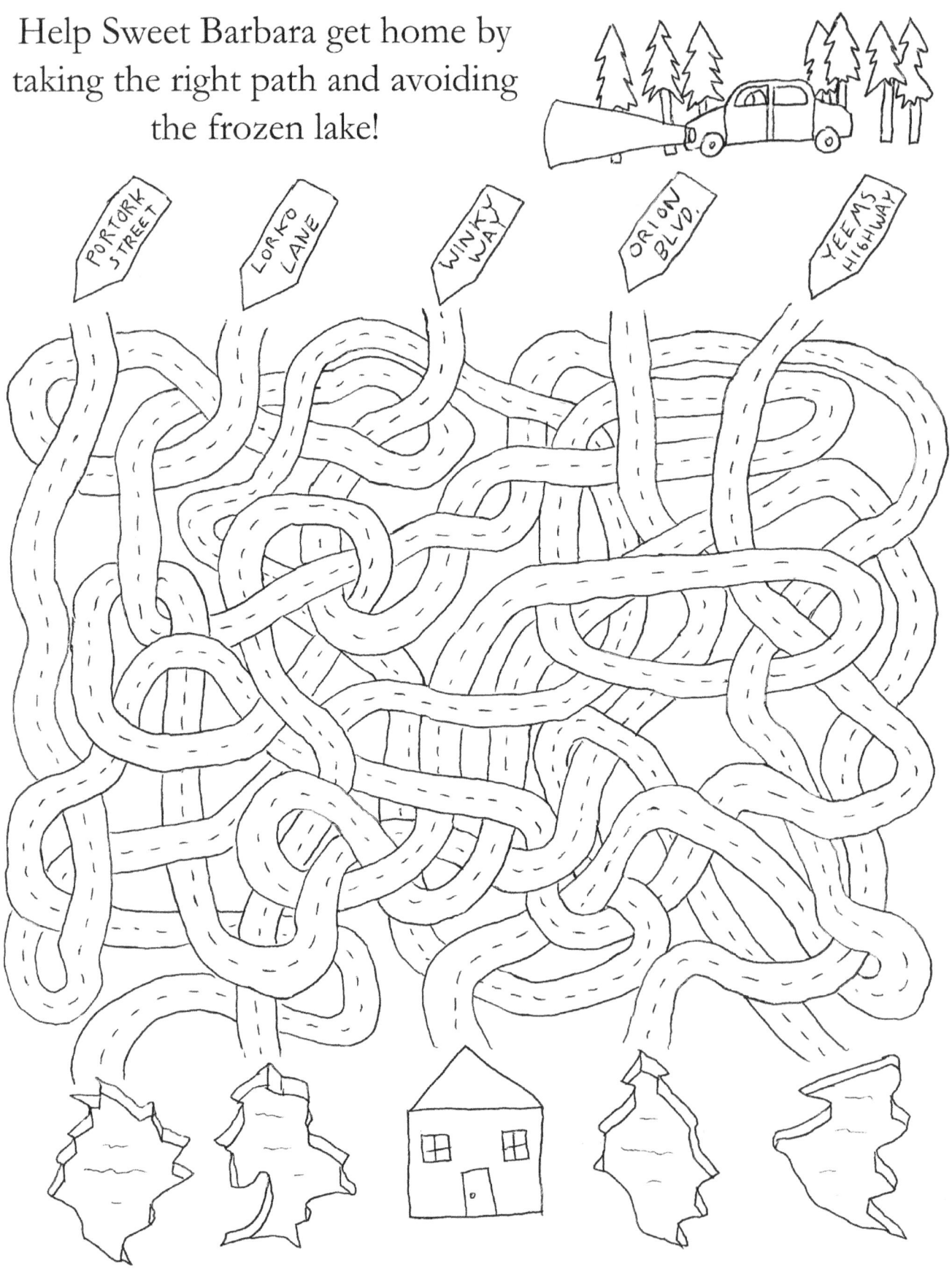

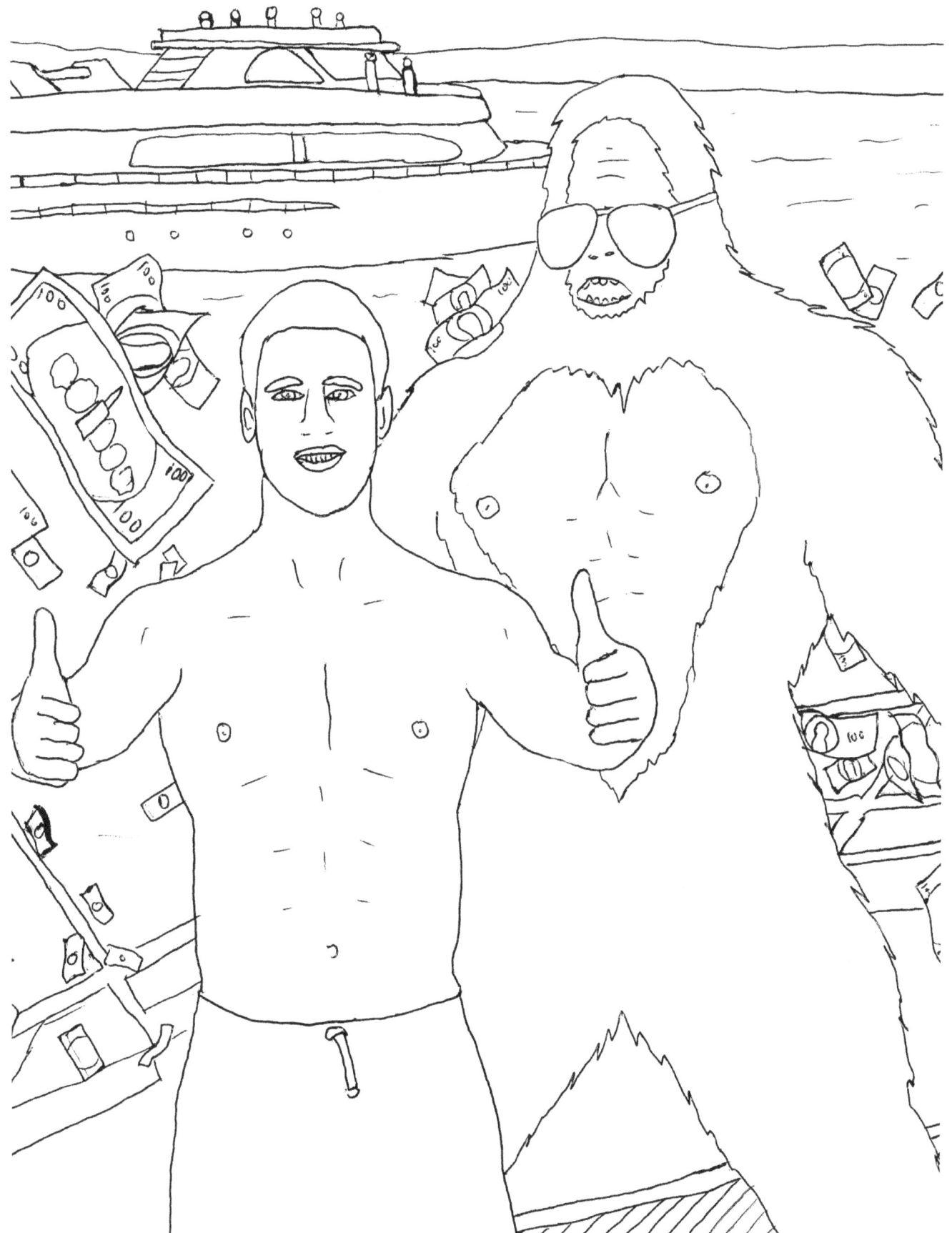

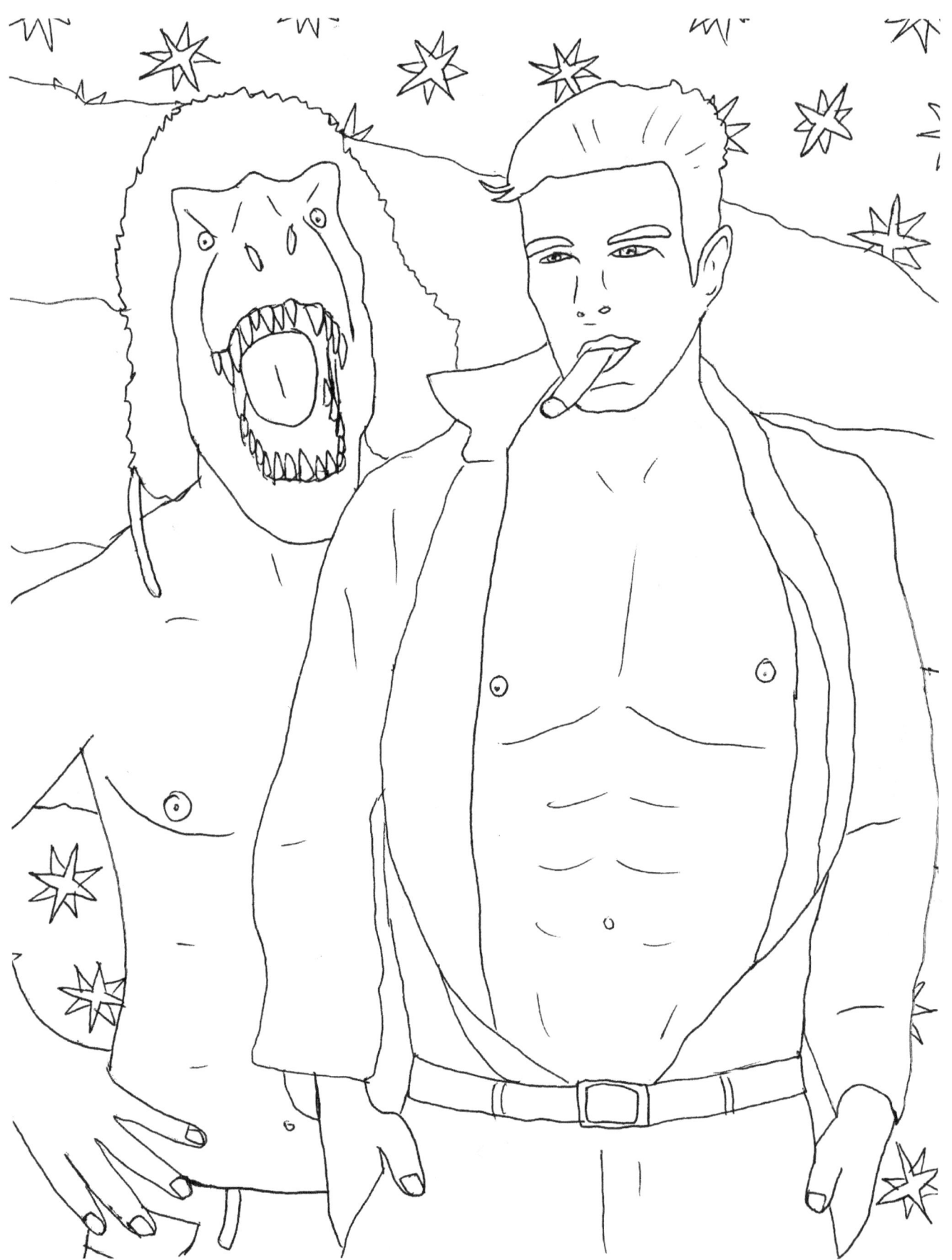

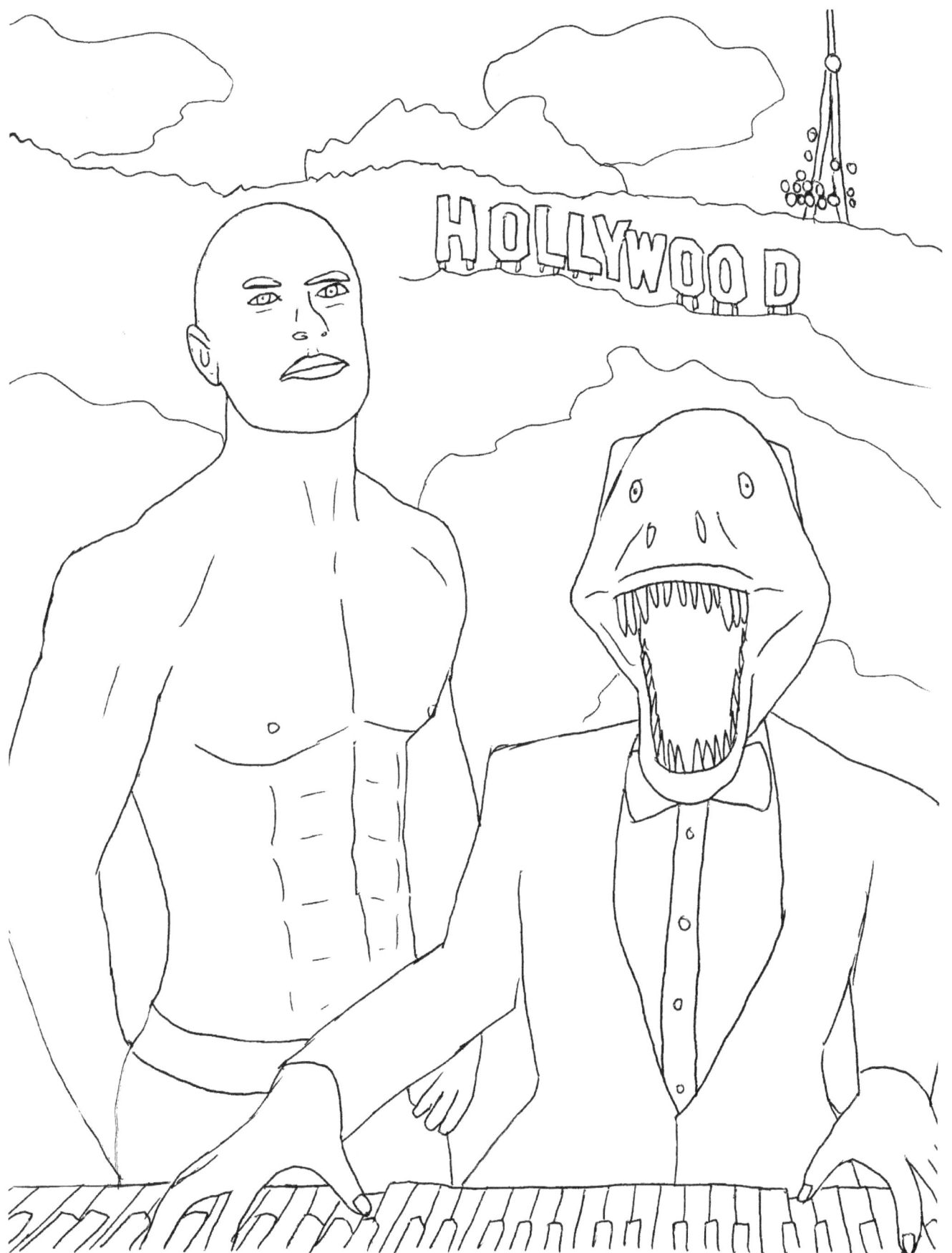

Use this space to draw an unspeakable cosmic horror of The Void.

Warning: Stop if Void Madness symptoms occur

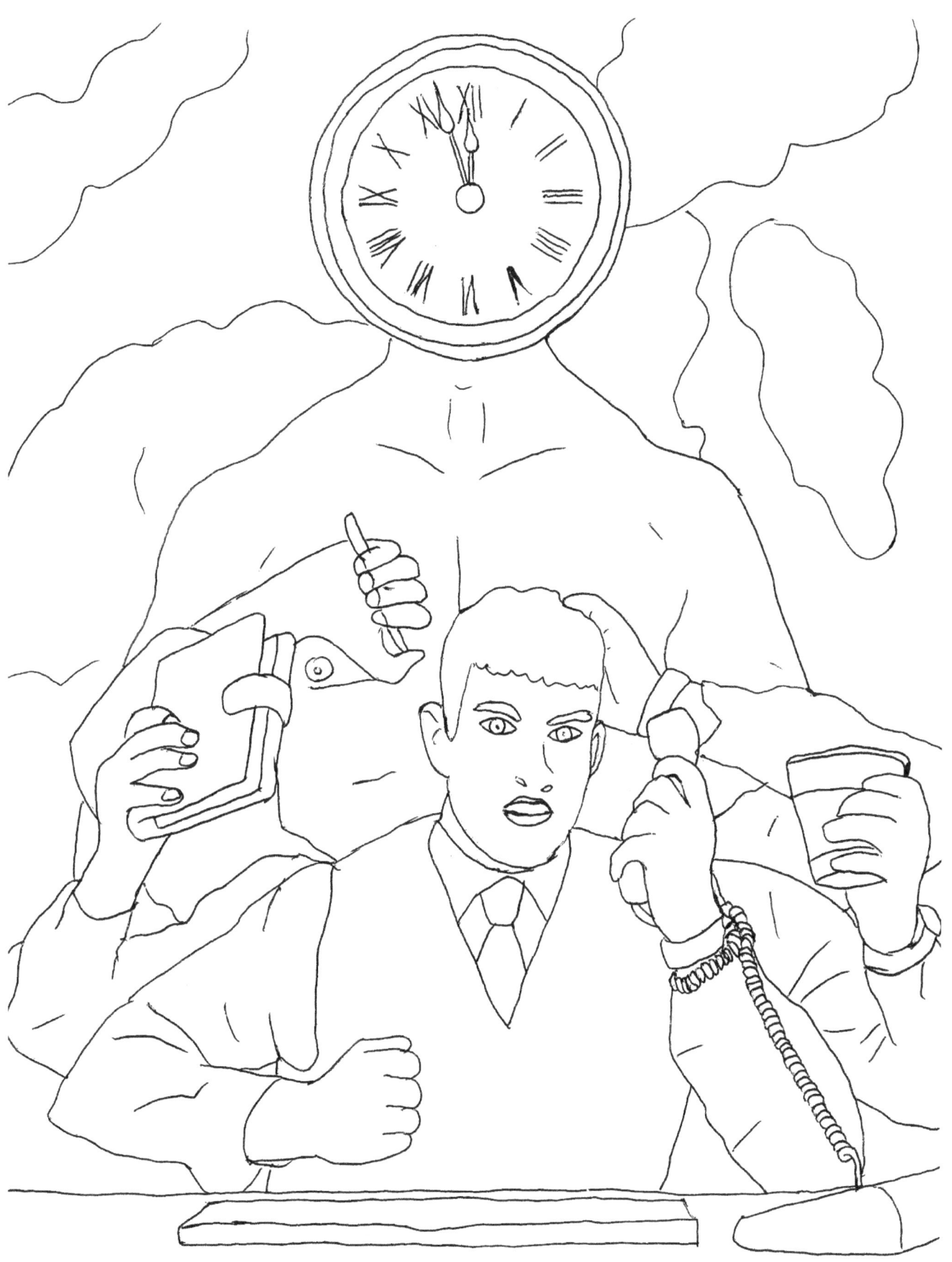

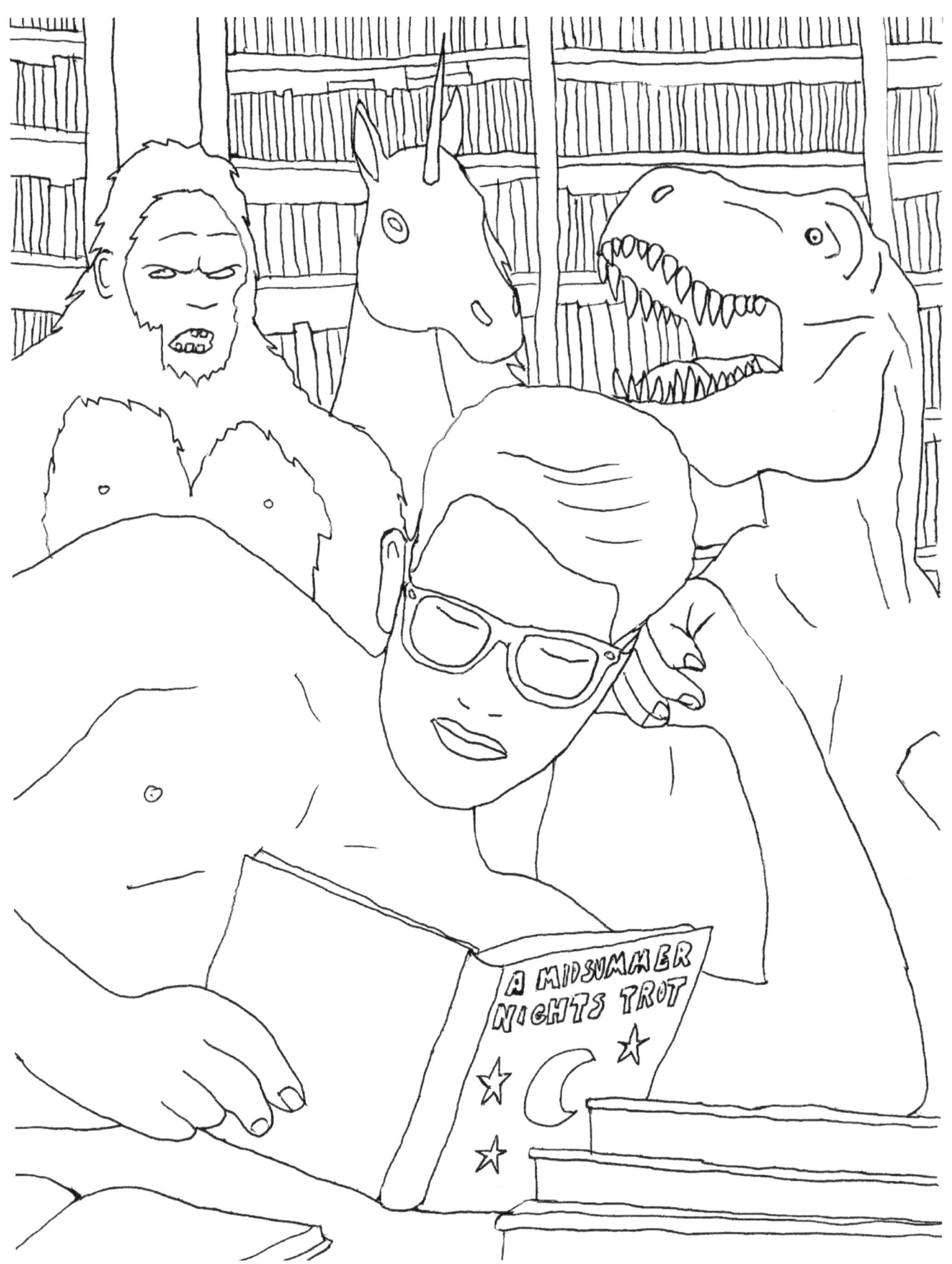

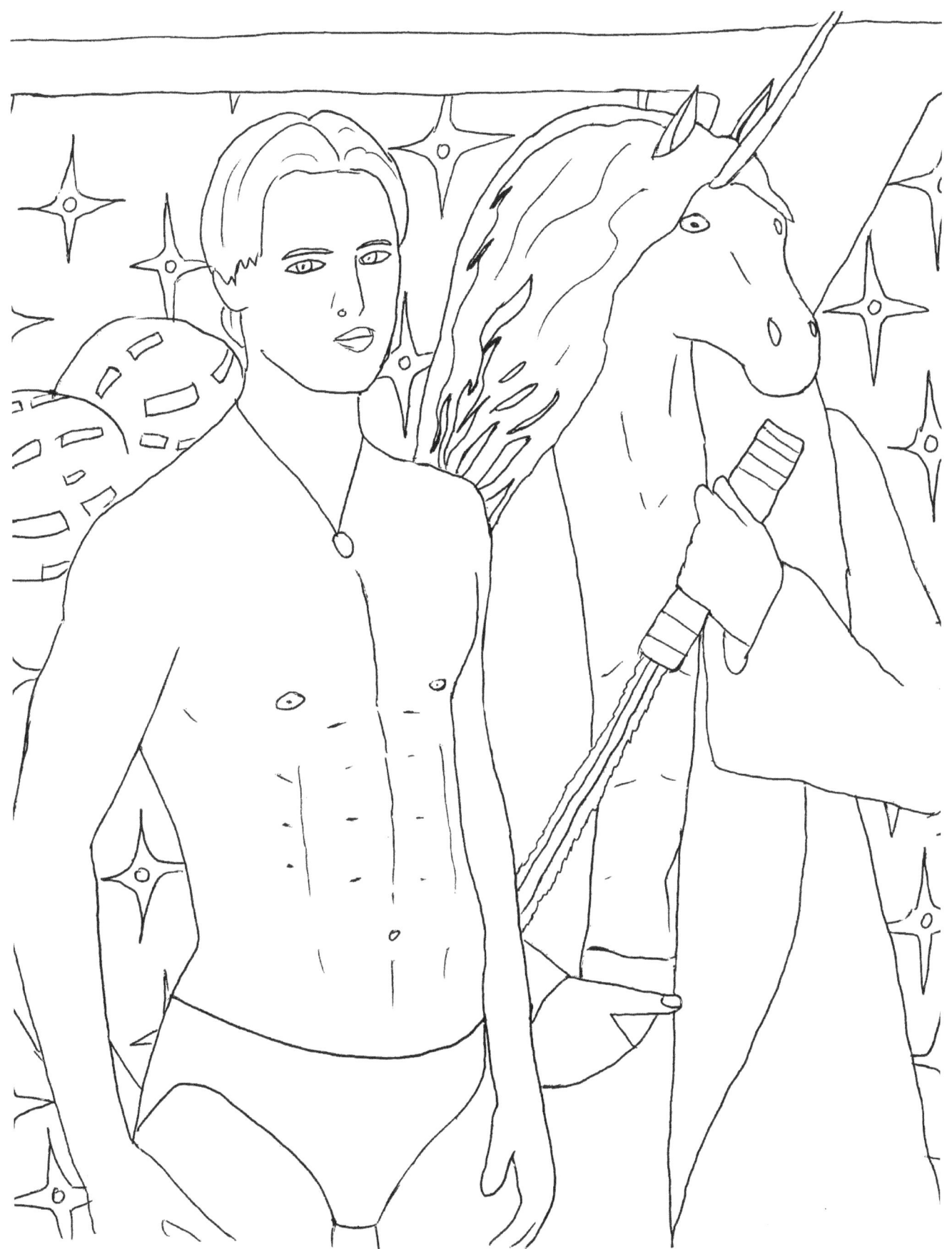

Use this space to draw your
dream bud.

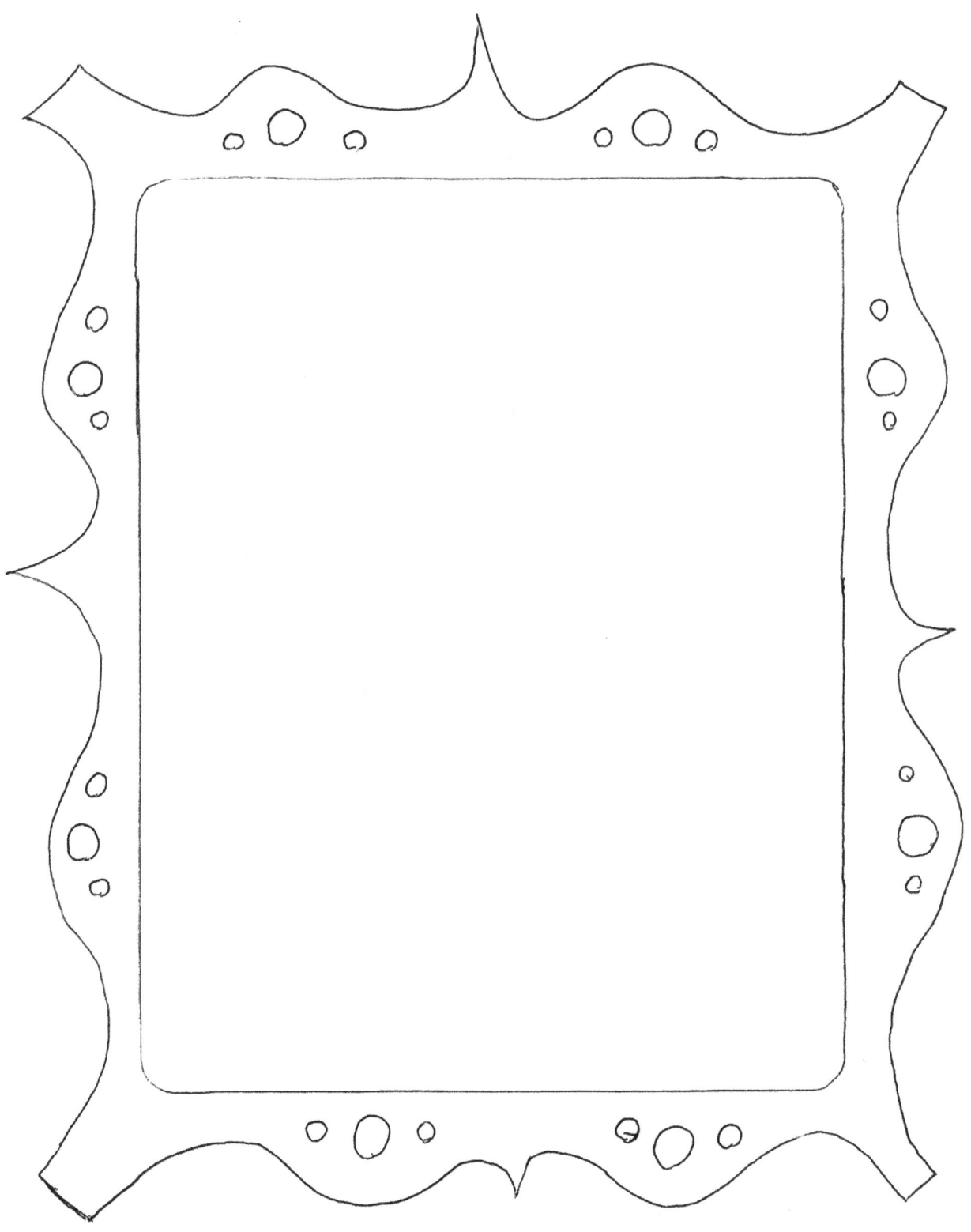

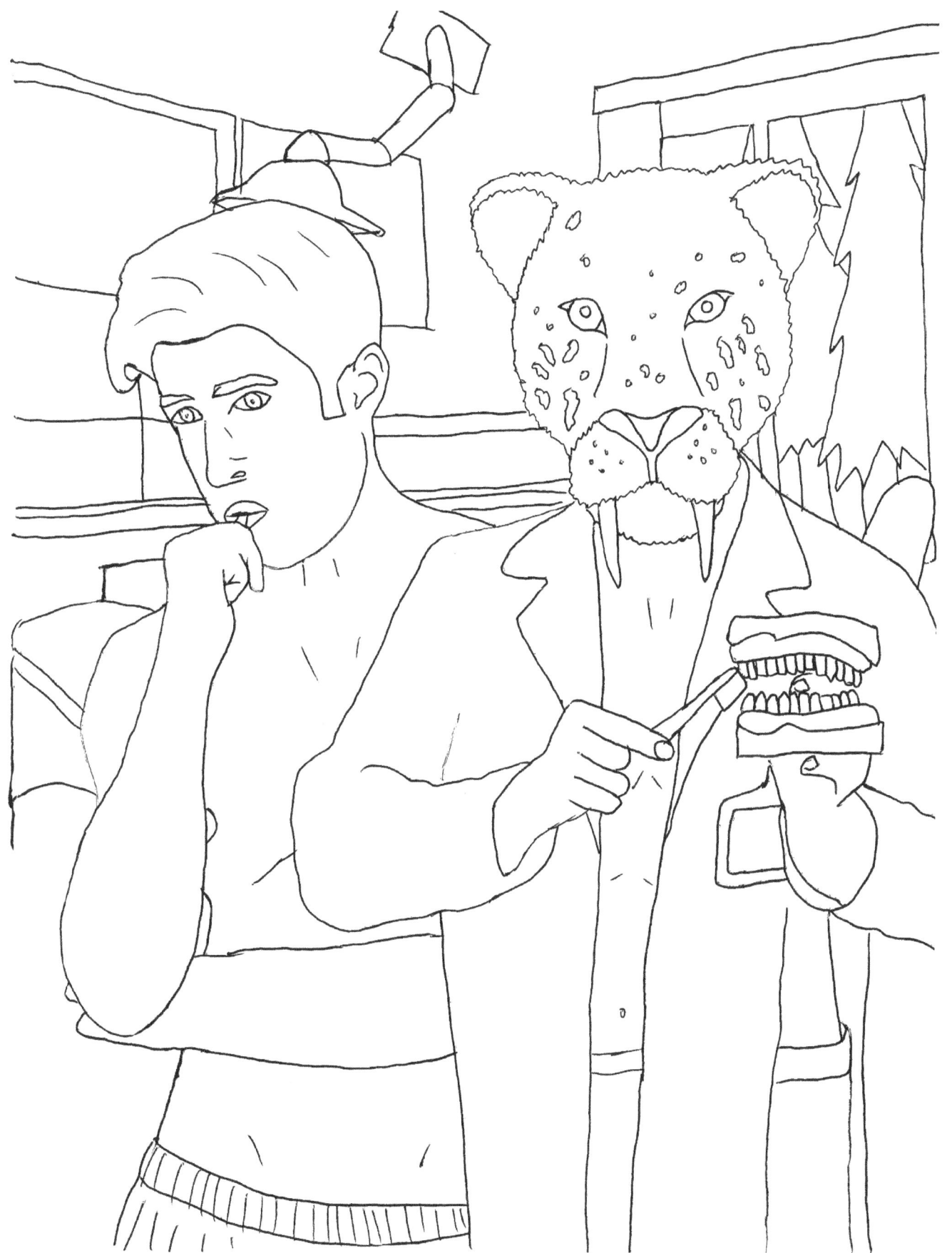

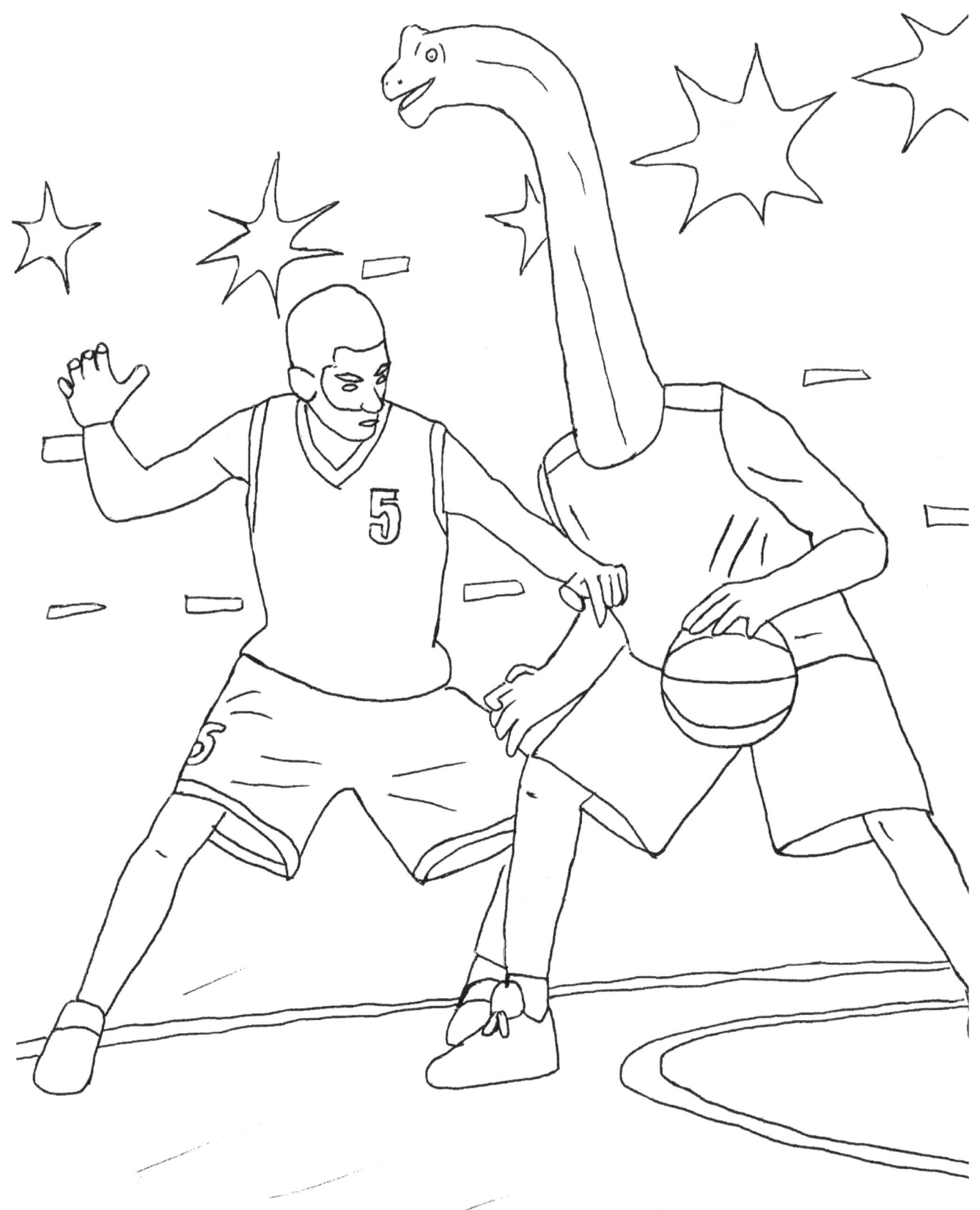

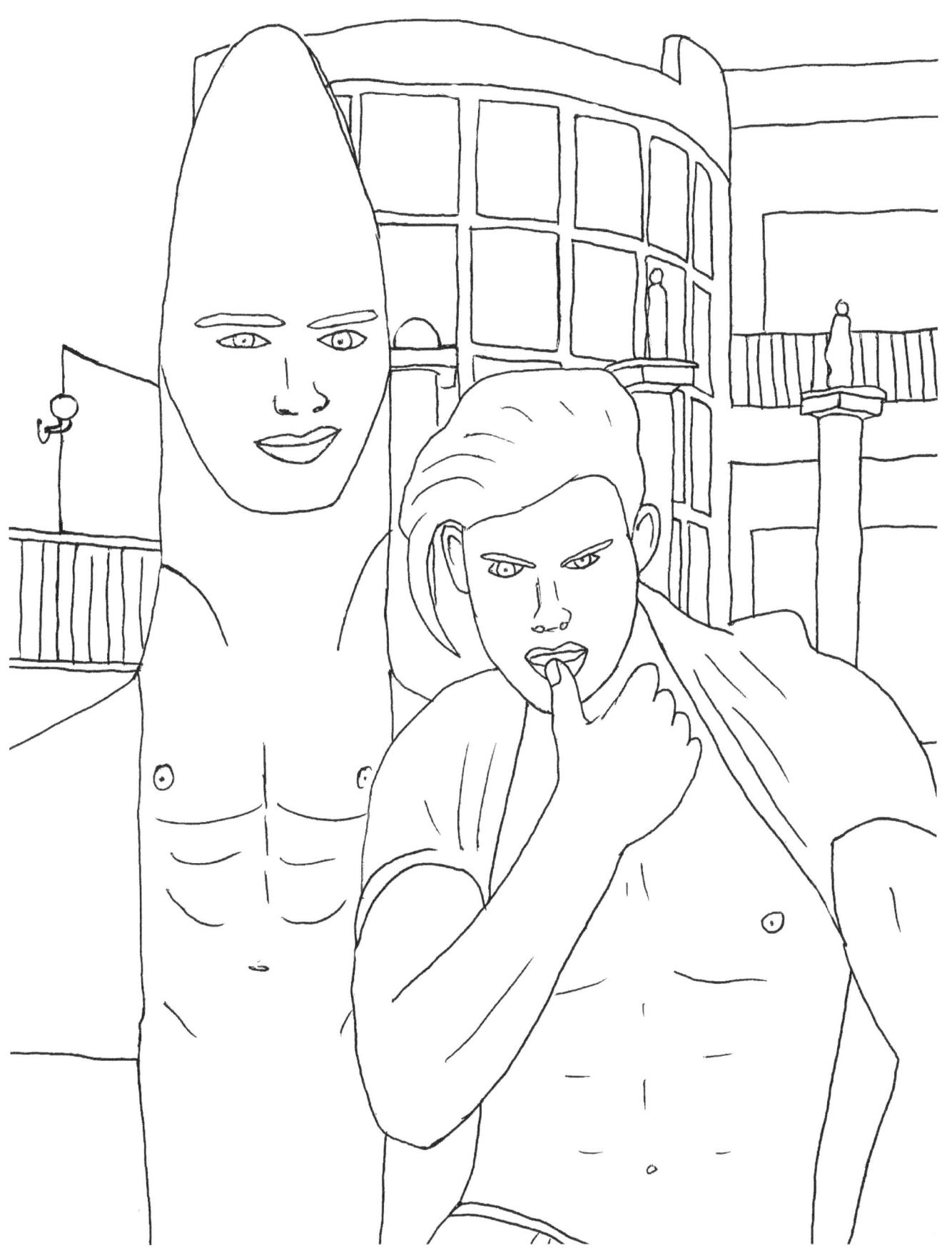

Help Davey Swimmer escape The Void!

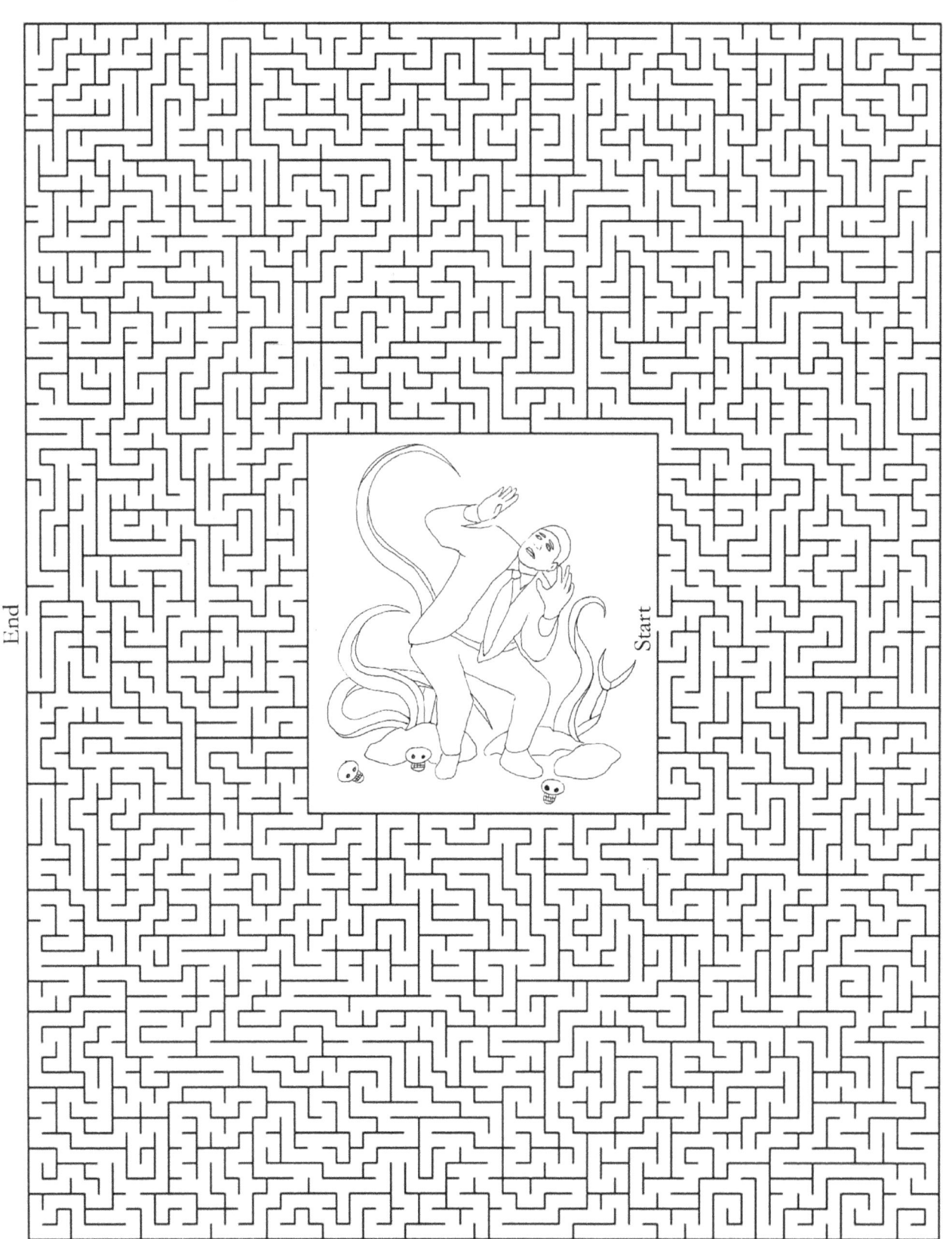

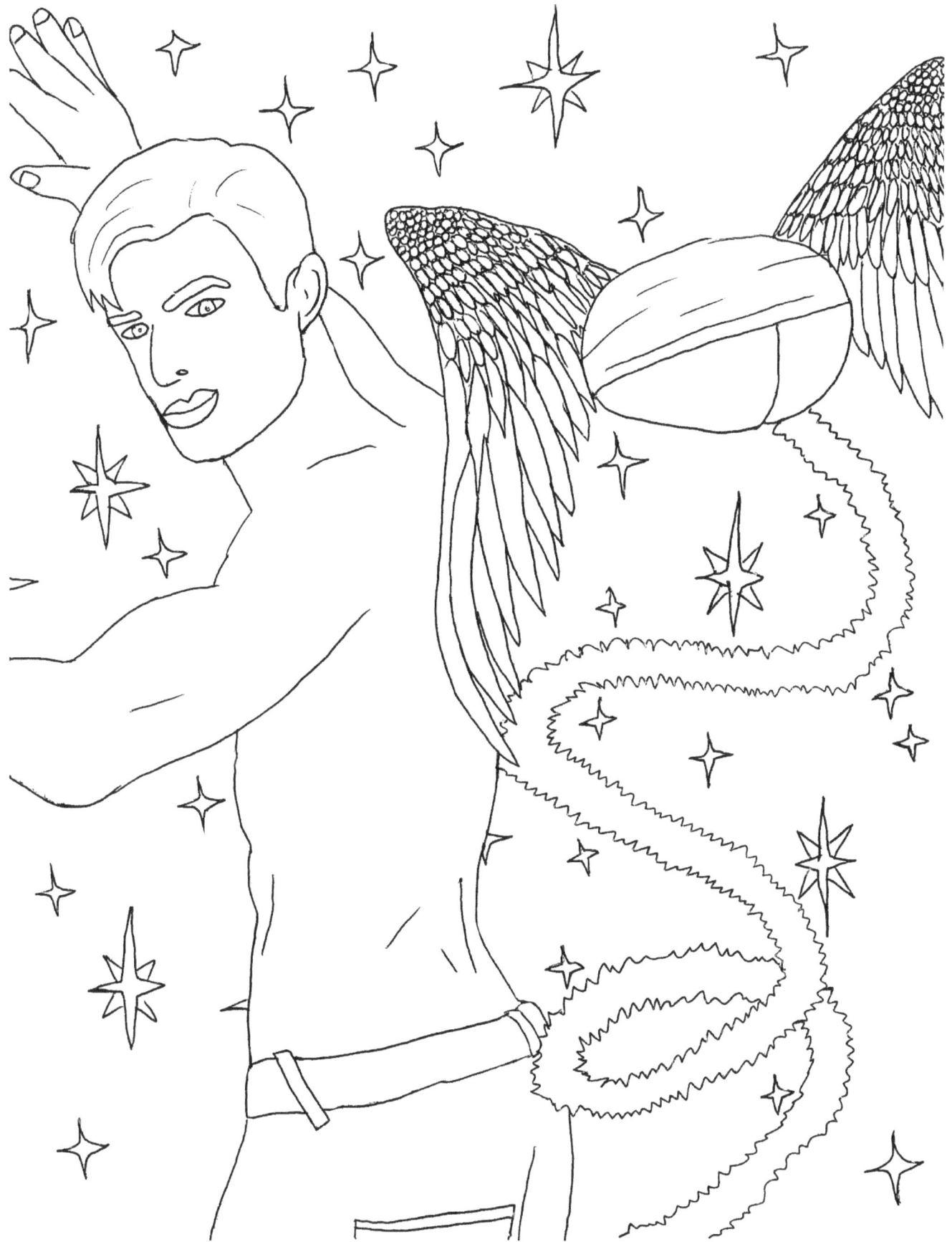

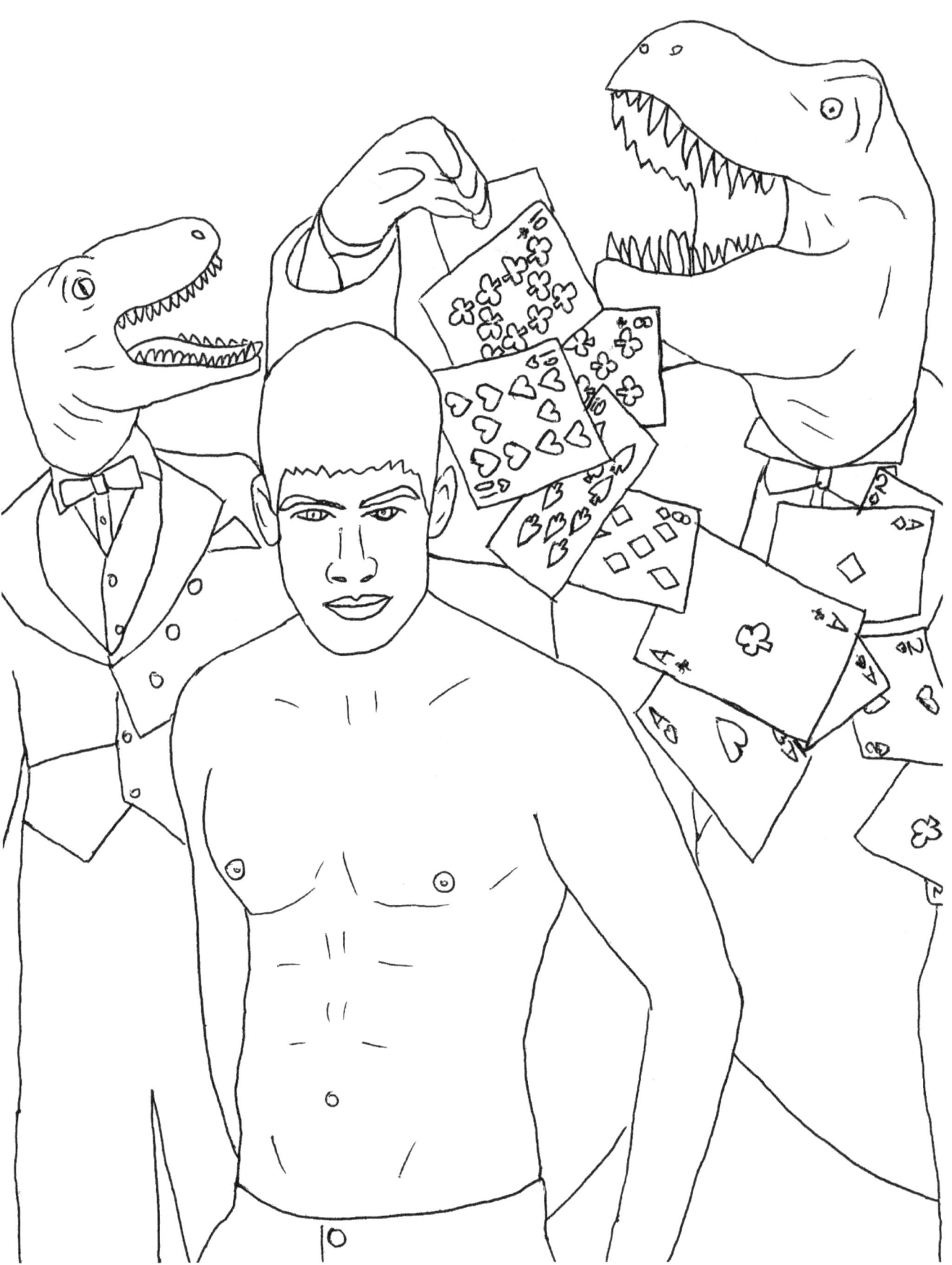

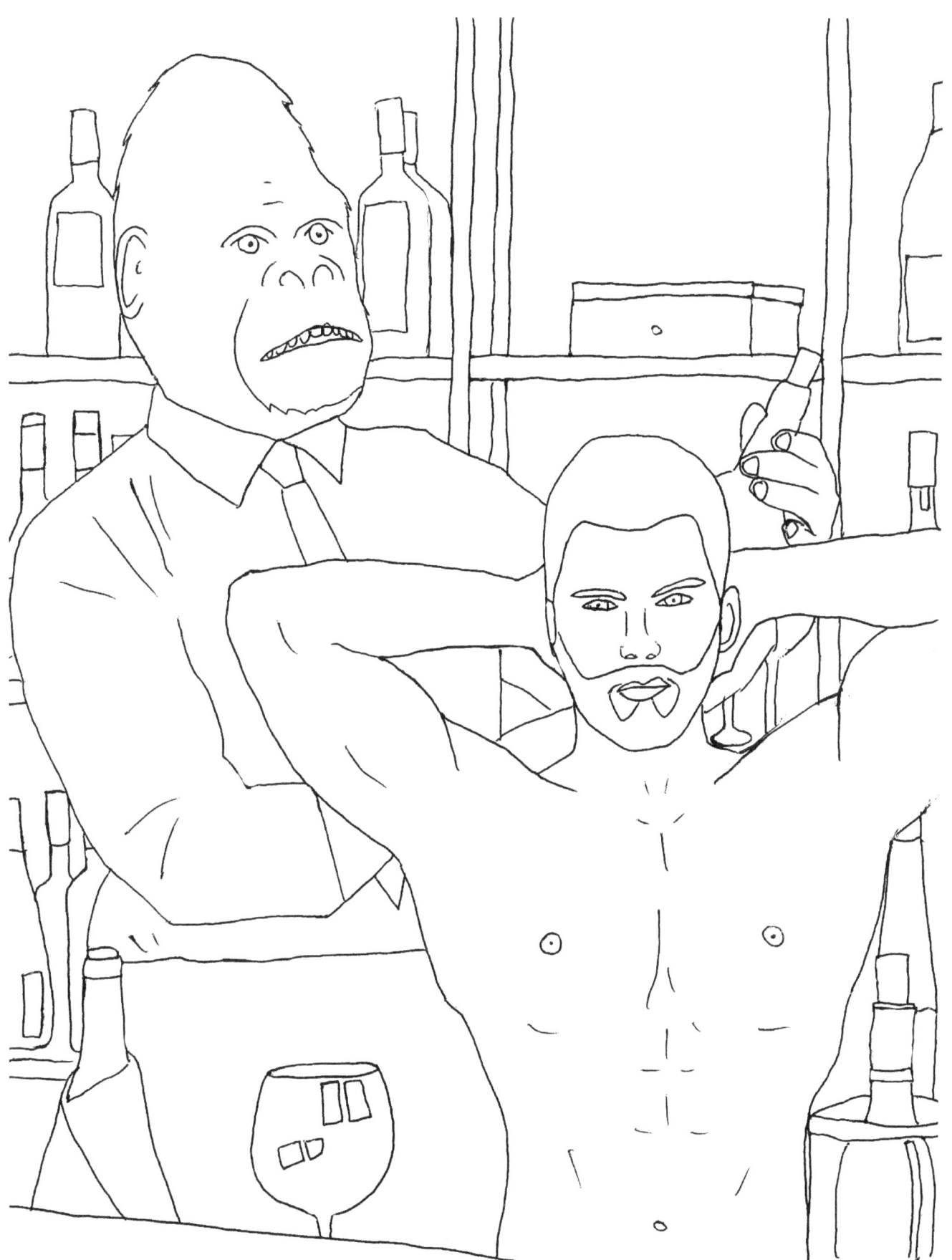

Can you help son (name of Jon) edit Chuck's lastest Tingler by finding the hidden words in the scrambled letters below? Look forward and backward, horizontal, diagonal or vertical to reveal the buckaroo phrases and help finish Dr. Tingle's latest masterpeice before it becomes old news.

```
G K L I V I N G O B J E C T K C U H C C W H T
B I G F O O T Z T T X H P D E V I L M A N H Z
L H O O R A K C U B I M A R B L E S P U Q V C
O T I M E L I N E S W N D R V O I D Z R Y T U
N B H O R S E P L A Y C G F D B K J U O U R N
E V C C M V E V B T L E T L R B T P A M D U B
S T G Z A N B I L L I N G S E O U J T A Y C A
O S E V L A C P O U N D E D I V Z D H N W K R
M L Q D T I P E K A N S F Y L D E E S C O M B
E I X L R B C O B B L E R E B O M R N E L A A
S P A C E R A P T O R B F G B I A B S L C N R
S D F U S C O U N D R E L U F I H B I E A F A
S S T B L A E R S I E V O L B U T T W D M K H
N N O R U A S O N I D C R N E M O S D N A H E
L N R S Z G D A E R D C I M S O C E T X U U L
G N T Q E S O N J O N U N I C O R N I N G U F
```

BARBARA	COBBLER	LIVINGOBJECT	SONJON
ROMANCE	SPACE RAPTOR	SCOUNDREL	COSMIC DREAD
BUCKAROO	HORSEPLAY	TINGLEVERSE	DINOSAUR
LONESOME	BILLINGS	MARBLES	LOVE IS REAL
BUTT	FROZEN LAKE	POUNDED	VOID
BIGFOOT	DEVILMAN	COBBLER	TIMELINE
CLOWY	TRUCKMAN	SNAKE PIT	UNICORN
CHUCK	HARD BUDS	HANDSOME	TROT

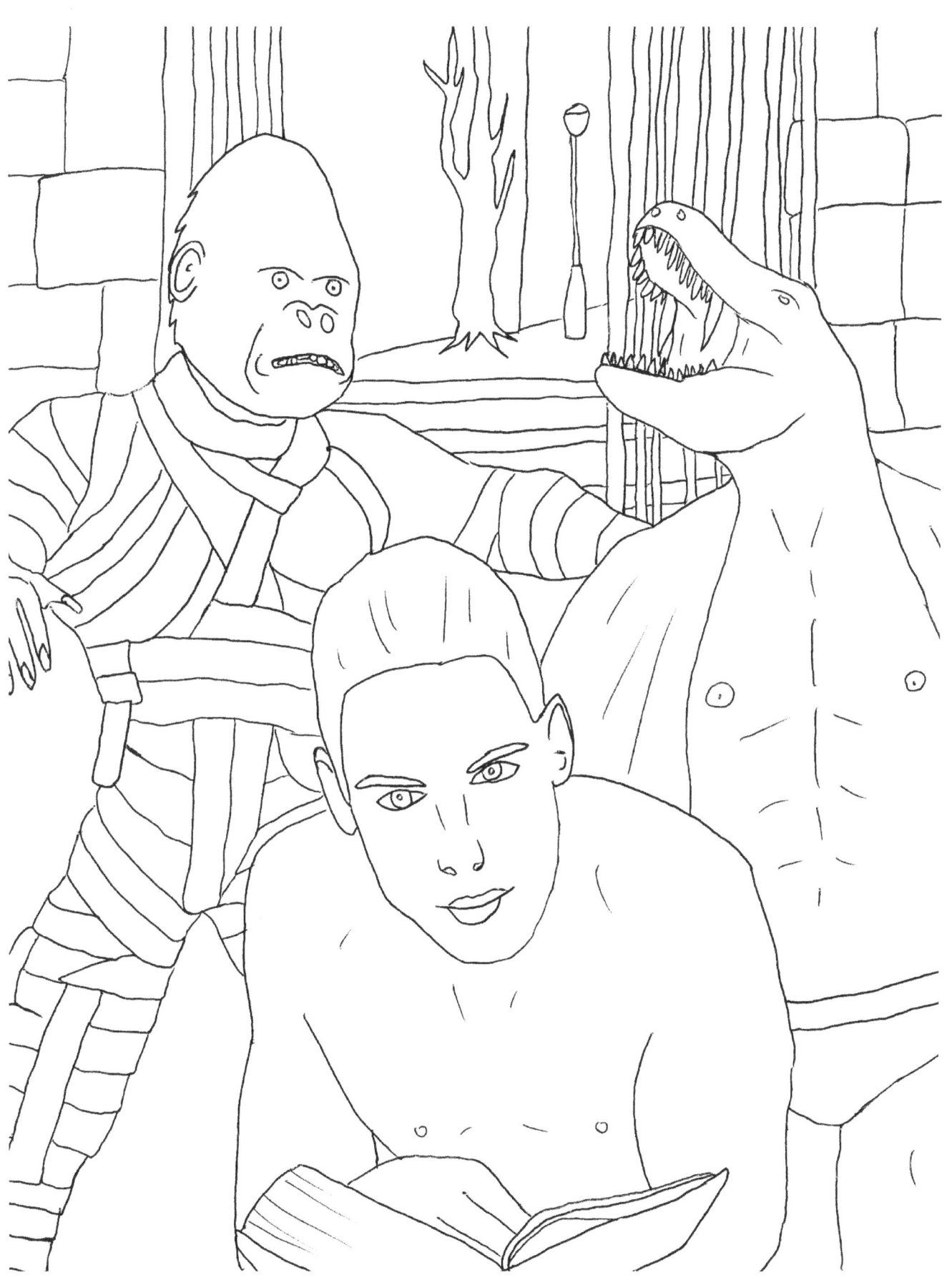

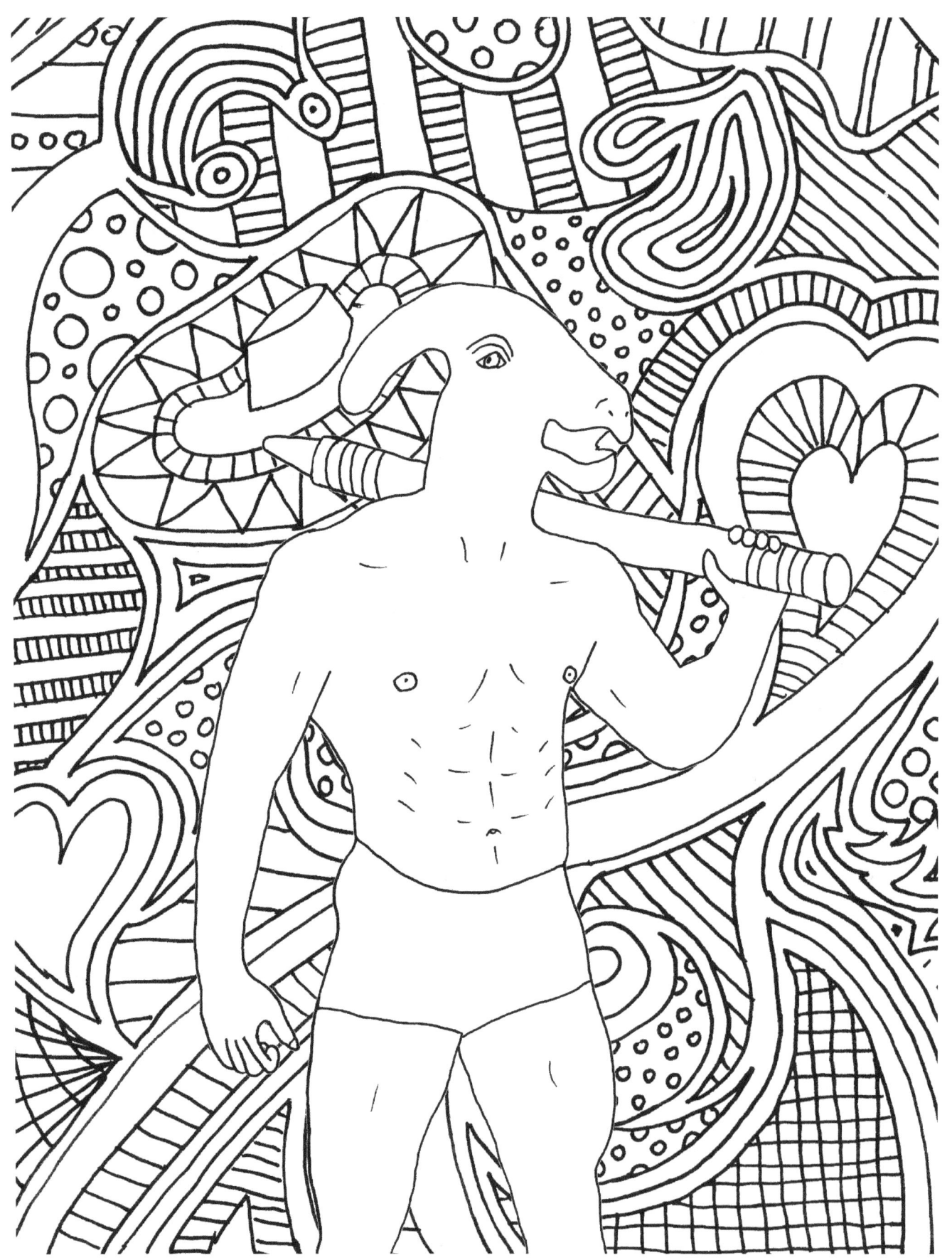

Solutions:

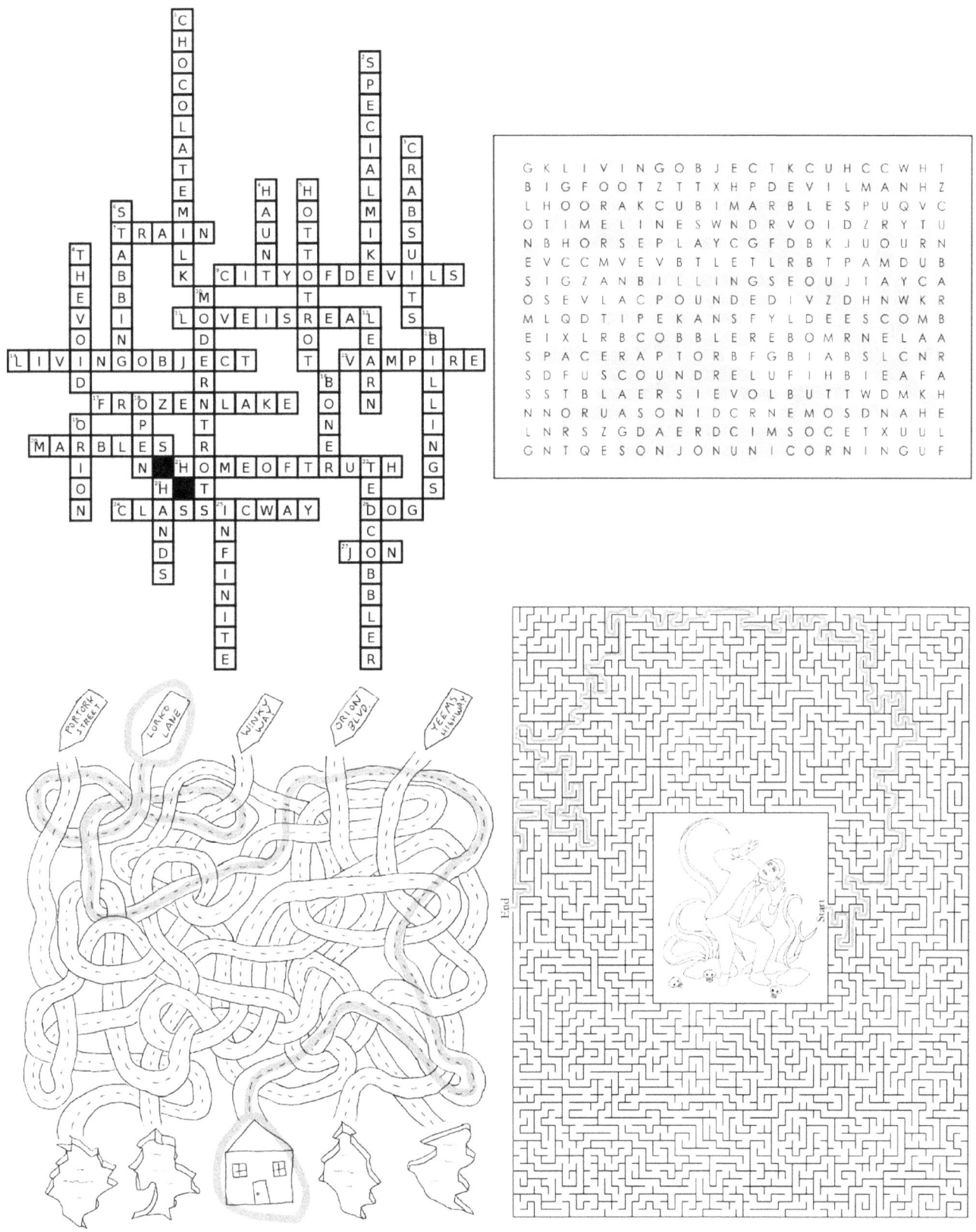

ABOUT THE AUTHOR

Two time Hugo Award finalist, Dr. Chuck Tingle, is an erotic author and Tae Kwon Do grandmaster (almost black belt) from Billings, Montana. After receiving his PhD at DeVry University in holistic massage, Chuck found himself fascinated by all things sensual, leading to his creation of the "tingler", a story so blissfully erotic that it cannot be experienced without eliciting a sharp tingle down the spine.

Chuck's hobbies include backpacking, checkers and sport. He is also a prominent flavor rights activist and the creator of the non-profit advocacy group, Allow All Flavors.